BITE-SIZED
BOOKS

A Bite-Sized Business Book

Why You Should Welcome Customer Complaints

(and what to do about them)

Nigel Greenwood
Simply Customer Ltd
www.simplycustomer.co.uk

Published by Bite-Sized Books Ltd 2015

Bite-Sized Books Ltd
Cleeve Croft, Cleeve Road, Goring RG8 9BJ UK
information@bite-sizedbooks.com
Registered in the UK. Company Registration No: 9395379

Contents

Introduction

The title of this book may sound strange — why on earth would a business want to welcome complaints, especially given the cost of dealing with them and any compensation that needs to be paid?

Well, I think complaints are one of the best opportunities for a business to learn from its customers, to make changes so they are delivering what they want, and to build a lasting, profitable relationship.

Why? Research shows that only 4% of customers will tell a business if they are not happy with their product or service. That means that, unless you have a process in place to regularly gather feedback from customers, you simply don't know what you need to start or stop doing to win more customers and keep them for longer. That means that those customers who care enough to complain, are a great source of information.

Not only that, if you handle the complaint properly, they are likely to become a real advocate of your business and will generate referrals for you:

- Happy customers who get their issue resolved tell about 4-6 people about their experience. — *White House Office of Consumer Affairs.*

So that's why you should welcome complaints (and handle them properly) — it's an opportunity to learn and to turn customers into real advocates of your business. If you don't get many complaints, you need to have a process for gathering customer feedback (see my next book!) so they have the opportunity to tell you what changes they want to see — understanding what your customers want, how they want it and how much they want to pay for it then delivering all of that is the quickest way to grow a profitable business!

Chapter 1

Why Customers Complain

At first glance, it may seem that there are numerous reasons why customers complain. For example, utility companies and banks in the UK often publish their top 10 reasons why their customers complain (and that's only the tip of the iceberg!), but actually there are only 3 main reasons:

1. Price – this can be any of:

a) Your product or service is more expensive than they thought it would be.

You can prevent this type of complaint by making sure you communicate as clearly as possible. I recently tried to join a local Chamber of Commerce. Their website listed 4 types of membership, and the features of each – but I didn't find out the price until I filled in the application form! I cancelled straightaway as it was much more expensive than I thought it would be.

Always remember that price is one of the features of your product, and make sure it is as clear as possible to the customer. Some businesses don't do this because they think it will put prospective customers off – but the opposite is true – my wife gets annoyed at me when I won't go into a jewellery store that doesn't display their prices but I explain that not showing the prices means that I won't be able to afford them!

Think as well about the total price the customer will pay. A good example of this is the budget airlines such as EasyJet and Ryanair – they attract customers by advertising a low price, but there are a number of hidden costs such as seat selection, food and baggage costs which mean that often they are much more expensive than you expected!

b) You are more expensive than your competitors.

This is more about the perceived value for the customer. It's fine to be more expensive than your competitors if you can justify it, for example by the level of service or support, or any other additional features.

Food supermarkets in the UK are a good example. For years, Tesco and Sainsbury's were market leaders until food discounters such as Aldi and

Lidl entered the market and began to take market share by offering similar service at much lower prices. One food supermarket that wasn't affected was Marks & Spencer, who have higher prices but match them with a much higher level of service – their customers are happy to pay the higher price because they value the higher level of service.

Another example is Stella Artois who actually use the slogan "reassuringly expensive". They back this up with advertising which emphasises the quality of the product and the brewing process – a good way of getting customers to see the value in the higher price.

To prevent this type of complaint, you need to regularly compare your prices and level of service with your competitors – if you are more expensive, can you justify it? A local farm shop opened a café a few months ago so I took my wife for a coffee. I was amazed when they asked for £7.60 for 2 lattes when similar cafes would charge £4.80 at most – so I complained. The manager couldn't justify the higher price as they were no different to their competition. Interestingly, they now charge £2.40 for a latte but I haven't been back yet!

c) Customers don't think it offers enough value for the money they have paid.

Mainly this comes down to the way you promote your product or service and the promises you make. If you use phrases such as "long lasting", great taste", "quality service", "easy to operate" or similar then you need to make sure that you live up to them in your customers' eyes.

2) Product – this could be any of:
a) It doesn't do what you said it would –
Avoid the temptation to over promise to attract purchasers – you may get a higher number of sales initially but they will turn into complaints and lost customers!

b) The quality is not what they expected –
When you launch a product or service, get some friends to trial it and use their feedback to make sure it lives up to expectations.

c) It's harder to use than they thought –
I worked with a software provider who offered a 30 day free trial, and made it really easy to opt into the trial – you could sign up in less than a minute and start using the software without any training. This created the expectation that the software was really easy to use. Unfortunately, although it was excellent, it was difficult to use initially which generated a

lot of complaints and cancellations.

d) It breaks! –

Other than checking the quality of your products and services, and making sure you have very clear instructions, there isn't much you can do about this as it will happen occasionally. However, if you handle the complaint properly you will keep your customers happy!

3) Service – this is typically the reason for around 70% of customer complaints.

It's normally down to poor communication and broken promises (for more information see my book "The 6 things that all customers want"). If you continually review your service, ask for and analyse customer feedback, make changes and tell customers about them, then you should minimise this type of complaint.

To summarise, you can minimise complaints by regularly asking for customer feedback and by asking yourself the following questions:

PRICE:
1. Are we more expensive than competitors – if so can we justify it?
2. Do we make the total price clear early in the buying process?
3. Do we offer value for money – how do we know that?

PRODUCT:
1. Does the product or service do everything we say it will?
2. Does it meet customer expectations – how do we know that?
3. Is it as easy to use as we lead customers to expect – how do we know that?

SERVICE:
1. Do we keep the promises we make?
2. Is it easy for a customer to get information or help?
3. Do we tell customers what will happen, when and how?

Chapter 2

Why It's Important to Handle Complaints Properly

There has been a lot of research about how many customers will stop doing business with you if they don't feel you have handled their complaint properly and, on average, it's about half of them!

Not only that, but they will start to tell other people about their experience with you, which will impact your sales:

- A dissatisfied customer will tell between 9-15 people about their experience. Around 13% of dissatisfied customers tell more than 20 people. – White House Office of Consumer Affairs.

By the way, these figures were compiled before the massive expansion of social media – there is now a risk that a dissatisfied customer could tell thousands of people not to do business with you. One customer of United Airlines was on a plane waiting for take-off when he saw baggage handlers throwing his guitar case around before loading it. The guitar broke so he complained. After 9 months the Customer Relations Manager refused to compensate him. The musician said that he would write a song and post a video on Youtube. United's reaction was "good luck with that one pal". The musician (Dave Carroll) went ahead. When it started to attract a high number of views, United contacted him and offered a replacement guitar if he withdrew the video. Dave's answer was "good luck with that one pal!" At the time of writing, the video has been viewed over 15 million times, Dave has now written a book (United breaks guitars) and has been interviewed often on national television. Soon after the video went viral, United Airlines share price dropped by 10%, wiping $180m off the value of the company!

On a smaller but more personal scale, we recently had a family lunch for 15 at a local pub for my dad's birthday. We'd never been to the pub before, but it looked great from the website, talking a lot about great home cooked food and friendly service. Unfortunately the food was overcooked and the service very slow. We complained during the meal and were offered free tea and coffee but no actual apology or explanation. I spoke to the manager who wasn't really interested in listening to me, said they didn't use customer feedback forms when I asked for one and actually disagreed with some of my comments.

When I got home I decided to put a review on Trip Advisor – a one star review. A week later, 7 more people from our party had also put a one star review on and we estimate over 500 people have now read them. I'm not sure what impact the reviews have had, but last Sunday we drove past the pub at lunchtime and there were only 5 cars in the car park at what should have been their busiest time. So not only did the pub lose the chance of any repeat business from 15 customers, it probably also lost the chance to serve 500 other people!

I know there are some customers who will never be happy and who will always look to complain and get compensation whenever they can, but that's a very small minority of people. Most of us just want good service and a value for money product or service that does what we expect.

Given the huge potential risk of a dissatisfied customer using social media to have a large impact on your business, can you take the risk of not making sure you handle all complaints to the customers' satisfaction?

The rest of this book gives you details about how to handle complaints, but as a failsafe, whenever you are resolving a complaint for a customer, take a minute to put yourself in their shoes and ask yourself:

"If it was me who made this complaint, would I tell others that it was handled really well and that I was happy with the result, or would I be telling people how bad the business was either personally or through social media?"

Chapter 3

What Do Customers Want When They Complain?

Although every complaint is specific to the individual customer, and the actions needed to resolve it equally individual, there are 3 key things that a customer is looking for when they make a complaint:

1. They want you to listen to them:

Listening to the customer explain what has happened and the impact it has had on them helps them "let off steam", removing the initial emotion, and also shows that you care about how they feel.

It's important that you and your staff are active listeners. By that I mean that you shouldn't have a script or bullet points to follow because then you will be thinking about the next thing you have to say rather than concentrating on what the customer is saying. Don't interrupt the customer even if you disagree with what they are saying – interrupting will almost always annoy them and make the situation much more difficult to handle.

Here are some hints and tips on active listening:

Show the customer you are interested in what they are saying by using both verbal and non-verbal messages such as maintaining eye contact, nodding your head and using facial expressions, showing understanding by saying 'I see' or simply 'Mmm hmm' to encourage them to continue. By providing this 'feedback' the customer will usually feel more at ease and therefore communicate more easily, openly and honestly.

Remain neutral and non-judgmental, don't take sides or form opinions, especially early in the conversation. Active listening is also about patience - pauses and short periods of silence should be accepted. Don't jump in with questions or comments every time there are a few seconds of silence. Active listening means giving the customer enough time to explain their thoughts and feelings.

Maintain eye contact if possible - It is normal and usually encouraging for the listener to look at the speaker. Eye contact can however be intimidating, especially for more shy speakers – gauge how much eye contact is appropriate for each customer.

Your posture can tell the customer a lot about whether or not you are really listening to them. An attentive listener tends to lean slightly forward or sideways whilst sitting. Other signs of active listening may include a slight slant of the head or resting the head on one hand.

Mirroring or reflection of any facial expressions used by the customer can be a sign of attentive listening. These reflective expressions can help to show sympathy and empathy in more emotional situations. This does need to be natural though – don't force it!

Don't appear distracted - no looking at a clock or watch, doodling, or anything else other than listening and taking notes.

Demonstrate that you have been paying attention by asking relevant questions and/or making statements that build or help to clarify what the customer has said. Ask things such as "so what happened was" or "and by that you mean..."

Repeating or paraphrasing what the customer has said is a good way to show that you understand.

Clarify anything you are not sure about by asking the customer open questions – these are ones which begin with who, how, what, where or when and encourage the customer to give a full answer rather than just say yes or no.

When the customer has finished speaking and you have asked enough clarifying questions to believe you dully understand the complaint, repeat back to them a summary of what they said in their own words. Summarising involves taking the main points of the complaint and reiterating them in a logical and clear way, using the customer's own words where possible so they don't think you are putting your own 'spin' on it and gives them the chance to correct you if necessary.

<u>2. They want you to show empathy:</u>

I've deliberately used empathy rather than an apology for 2 reasons.

First, some businesses I've worked with told their employees never to apologise. At first I thought it very strange, but then they explained that it was a legal point and that, by apologising, they could be seen as accepting responsibility and therefore liable for any compensation. Whilst I can understand their logic, it still doesn't help the customer or get the problem sorted out any faster!

The second reason is that empathy is far more powerful than an apology. When taking a complaint from a customer, showing empathy means:

- Apologising that the customer has had to complain (this is very different from apologising for the cause of the complaint),
  - Actively listening
  - Asking relevant questions to make sure you understand the issue (this shows the customer that you care)
  - Using their words wherever possible
  - Making it clear that you understand their point of view and the problems it has caused for them
  - Explaining that you want to help sort it out and then clearly explaining to the customer how their complaint will be handled (this sets their expectations).

3. They want resolution:

Put simply, the customer wants the problem sorting out, so they are in the same position that they would have been in had it not happened, and reassurance that it won't happen again. Normally this includes someone taking ownership of the problem, investigating why it happened and what the impact has been for the customer, communicating back to the customer at agreed points, offering a solution that means the customer hasn't been disadvantaged in any way, confirming that the customer is happy, apologising again and then starting the process to deliver any changes that are required to make sure it doesn't happen again.

It's really important to deliver all 3 of these:

I've been a customer of East Coast Trains for a long time, and have built up a number of loyalty points which I use to get free tickets from time to time. East Coast is now run by Virgin and they are closing the loyalty point scheme, so I logged on to the website recently to book some free tickets to take my wife to London for a day out. Having checked that I had enough points and that tickets were available for the day I wanted to travel, I went to 2 other sites, booked tickets to a theatre and reserved seats at a restaurant.

Then I went back to the Virgin site to book the train tickets. Instead of seeing the number of points, there was a message saying they couldn't check them at the moment and please try again later. Two hours later it was still the same message so I called.

From an empathy point of view the member of staff was great to a point– they apologised that I had to complain, listened to me, asked some questions so they understood the impact (if I couldn't get the free tickets I would have to pay £180). Unfortunately that's when it went downhill – they couldn't offer any help, I just had to wait until the site was fully functional again and no, they didn't know when that would be – I'd just have to keep checking. They didn't even offer to call me when the site was working again!

Looking for some form of resolution, I asked if they could book the tickets for me over the phone – no. Would they compensate me if I had to pay for tickets – I would have to talk to Head Office and they may consider some form of compensation!

I checked the site twice a day for 7 days and eventually got the tickets, but I've lost a lot of faith in Virgin. Unfortunately they are the only provider I can use to quickly get to London, so I don't have a choice – but if I had, I'd switch to another train company!

Contrast this with the service my wife received when a pair of earrings she ordered online arrived and one was broken – even though they had been packaged well. When she phoned, the member of staff was great – "I'm really sorry you've had to phone – I know how annoying this is when it happens". Then she asked if my wife needed them for a special occasion and explained that she would send a replacement pair that day by special delivery, even checking which was the best address to send them to. My wife got the replacement pair the next day with a small bag of sweets as an apology and the member of staff phoned that evening to confirm she had received them. Guess where my wife buys most of her jewellery from now?

Questions to ask yourself:

1. What do we say when someone phones to complain – do we actively listen and show empathy?
2. Do we do all the work when someone complains or does the customer have to do some of it?

Chapter 4

Taking Ownership of a Complaint

A customer has contacted you and complained, and you've listened and shown empathy. The next step is to take ownership. So what does that mean?

Well, ideally it means that the person who took the complaint from the customer has enough responsibility and authority to resolve it to their satisfaction whilst they are talking to them.

In a small business that can be easy, but becomes more difficult as your business grows. Once you employ staff who will be in contact with customers, you need to make sure that they have the necessary skills, experience and authority to handle most complaints (as well as training them in everything else they need to do!).

So how do you do that?

First, I'd explain to them that you are going to give them responsibility for handling complaints whenever possible and that you will give them the training, support and authority they need. Make it clear that you don't expect them to handle every complaint and have a clear process for them to follow when they come across one that they can't handle.

Second, explain to them what active listening is and allow them to practice in a safe environment, giving them feedback and coaching until you (and they) are happy that they are sufficiently skilled.

Third, explain to them what types of complaints they may get and what they are able to do about each one. This normally includes giving your staff limits on how much they can offer as a refund or compensation or how much they can spend on a gift to apologise, as well as information about your processes and timescales so they can set the customer expectations properly if the complaint can't be resolved immediately.

Fourth, arrange for them to practice handling complaints in a training environment – make sure they get constructive feedback and can practice until they feel confident in handling complaints.

Finally, let them start to handle complaints. It's important that initially you or another qualified person is available to support them. It's a bit like passing your driving test – they know and have demonstrated the skills required, but it's still a bit scary when you go out on the road without your L plates on so it's good to have someone by your side for the first few times!

If it's not possible to resolve the customer's complaint immediately, there are 4 key steps to taking ownership:

1. Explain that their complaint needs to be investigated to find out what has happened and give the customer the name and contact details of the person who will be dealing with their complaint
2. Explain clearly to the customer what will happen and when
3. Agree with the customer when and how you will update them until their complaint is resolved.
4. The named person should be responsible for ensuring that the complaint is fully investigated and that any promised timescales are met.

Questions to ask yourself:

1. Am I confident that my staff can handle most customer complaints themselves?
2. Do customers ever have to chase us about their complaint – if so, why?
3. If I had a complaint about my business, would I be happy with the way it was handled?

Chapter 5

Investigating a complaint

If you've received a complaint and haven't been able to resolve it immediately, it's normally because you need to do some investigation.

There are a few points to bear in mind:

1) It needs to be done with an open mind. At this stage, you don't know if the complaint is justified or not. The famous saying "the customer is always right" is not always the case! Although, even if the customer has a history of continually complaining, that doesn't mean that they do not have grounds for this complaint.

The purpose of the investigation is not to apportion blame, it's to establish the facts, to understand how the customer was affected so you can get a resolution that's acceptable to both the business and the customer, and to learn how to stop it happening again.

2) It needs to be documented, with any timescales promised to the customer being kept to. Remember as well to document how it was resolved, especially any compensation paid to the customer. This is partly to protect you against any further action by the customer, but mainly so you have notes to refer back to if it happens to another customer (especially if you find that other customers have been affected by the cause of the complaint during your investigation) so you can quickly get resolution and treat all affected customers fairly and consistently.

3) You need to find out the root cause so you can make sure any solution delivers lasting benefit in the right ways. This can be more complicated than it first appears it normally means continuing to ask why something happened (or didn't happen) until you are 100% confident that you know why.

Here's an example that happened to me recently:

We're gradually replacing all the lightbulbs in our house with LED bulbs as they last longer and are more energy efficient. We're doing it gradually because they are expensive!

I searched online for the type and size of bulb I wanted and chose one store's website. They had a lot of choice, and used dropdown boxes with multiple options for you to choose the number and type of bulb you wanted. Each dropdown box had a default option and every time you chose a different option the price altered accordingly. When I was ready to place my order, I went to the shopping basket but it showed my order as 6/12/round/candle/4w/6w bulbs. Confused, I deleted that and started again, double checking every time that I had chosen the right option. When I went to the basket again it showed the same as before so I assumed that was the way the system worked and placed the order.

When the bulbs arrived, they had sent 6 round bulbs instead of 12 candle bulbs – so I phoned and complained. They investigated and call me back to say that their records showed that was what I had ordered. I explained what had happened and asked them to check again. This time they called back to apologise – by continuing to investigate they had found a problem on their website functionality which meant that, when a customer ordered a specific number and type of bulb, a glitch in the system meant that the order reverted to the default selections.

I returned the incorrect order, got a refund and was about to reorder online when I thought it would be safer to phone.

When I called, I explained what had happened and asked if they had fixed the problem. They assured me that they had. But I then asked if they had tested any other variations of order – "No, why would we?" I pointed out that if it had happened in one scenario, it could happen in others and it was better to be proactive rather than wait for customers to tell them where something was going wrong. I haven't heard back from them but hopefully they are doing just that!

The point of this example is that a full investigation should always continue until the root cause has been established and the number of any customers affected known, otherwise you can continue to make similar mistakes which leads to frustrated customers, lost sales and ultimately extra cost for the business!

4) It's important to bear in mind that the customer could be complaining about something that HAS gone wrong, or something that they THINK has gone wrong. Although you may be confident that all your processes have worked exactly as they are supposed to, you may have over promised something in your marketing material – and that may have led to the complaint!

Finally, an investigation should be managed by one person. Although there may be several people investigating the complaint, always have just one person collating the results, producing a summary, communicating with the customer. Two reasons for this – management by committee almost always something takes longer to resolve, and it's incredibly frustrating for a customer to phone to check what's happening and to have to explain again what happened to someone who has just picked up their file!

Questions to ask yourself:

1) Does a customer always talk to the same person about their complaint?

2) Do we have detailed notes when we investigate a complaint?

3) Do we check if any other customers are affected?

4) Do we really get to the root cause of why a complaint happened?

Chapter 6

Communication – Why It's Important and How to Do It When Handling Complaints

When a customer feels they have cause to complain, it's because they have a problem. When they have made their complaint, they feel that it's now your problem and therefore you should sort it out.

In simple terms, they expect you to do all the work!

And by that they mean that you contact them with updates on progress – they should never have to chase you!

When you receive a complaint, if it's in person or over the phone, explain what you will need to do to investigate, how long it will take and how often you will keep them updated. Agree the frequency of updates and how you will update with the customer. Every time you contact them with an update, explain what will happen next and agree when you will update them again.

If you get a complaint in writing, always try to contact the customer by phone – it's much easier to get all the facts and set their expectations about what will happen and when, and often you will find that, however complicated the complaint appears to be, there is a simple answer and you can turn the customer into a happy one quite quickly.

On my first day as Head of Customer Loyalty for a major UK bank, I was surprised to see the Chief Executive heading to my desk. I was even more surprised when he explained that part of my role was to help him answer executive complaints, especially in areas where I had more knowledge than him. He then dropped a 5 page letter on my desk, saying "here is the first one – can you look into it and draft a reply for me by the end of the day".

I started to read the letter but found it really difficult to properly understand what the complaint was really about. After spending an hour trying to draft a reply, I wasn't getting anywhere so phoned the customer to try and find out what they wanted.

When I explained who I was and that the Chief Executive had personally asked me to look into his complaint, the customer thanked me for calling, saying that he was really surprised that we had taken the time to call but that he was really pleased because it showed we cared about our customers. After 10 minutes on the phone, I managed to resolve the complaint to his satisfaction and we parted, maybe not the best of friends, but on good terms.

I e-mailed the Chief Executive, explaining what I had done and that there was no need for any further action. Immediately I got a phone call from his PA who basically said that I hadn't followed the correct procedure and that, in future could I please just draft a suitable response!

I went home a little disheartened and brooded about it all weekend. When I arrived at work on the Monday, there was a note on my desk asking me to go to the Chief Executive's office as soon as I got in. Fearing for my job, I went straight away. When I got there he came out to greet me – "Nigel, I just wanted to thank you for phoning that customer – he has written to me thanking us for the way we handled his complaint. In future, please feel free to phone customers rather than draft a reply – anything that helps customers and cuts my workload down at the same time is brilliant in my eyes".

Clear, regular communication won't solve every case - you will still get customers grumbling if they think it is taking too long, but most will understand if you explain everything clearly so they can see that you are working in their best interests.

By taking the initiative and regularly updating customers, you will also remain in control of the situation – many businesses have more complaints about the complaint procedure that anything else, and most of those are that the customer has had to continually chase the business for updates.

And finally - think about the language you use – keep away from jargon and acronyms. They may be widely understood in your business or industry, but are unlikely to mean anything to a customer and they will probably just think that you are trying to hide something if you go into a long technical explanation.

Questions to ask yourself:

1. Do we agree with the customer when and how we will update them?

2. Do we phone if we get a written complaint?

3. Do we use jargon or technical terms that a customer is unlikely to understand?

Chapter 7

Getting a resolution with the customer

You've received a complaint, you've listened and confirmed you have all the facts, you've conducted an investigation and kept the customer updated.

You're now at the point where you're going to contact the customer to explain what you are proposing to do to set it right (this is where your nerves can start jangling!).

The first thing to do is to review your proposal, asking yourself 2 key questions:

1. Does it address all the points raised by the customer? – if yes, move to question 2, if no, then reconsider your proposal to see if you can address all the points. Ask yourself – if this had happened to me, would I be happy to accept this proposal?

2. Does your proposal put the customer in the same position that they would have been in if they hadn't had to complain? If no, reconsider (remember to include any stress or inconvenience caused). If yes, it's time to pick up the phone (always try to phone rather than write, but remember to confirm your proposal in writing once you have the customer's agreement to it). This is key. I spoke to a business owner recently who had ordered a piece of equipment they needed for a job on a specific date. It arrived broken so he phoned to complain. The supplier apologised and promised to send a replacement out. Their solution was to send 2 pieces of equipment. Unfortunately they arrived a day late and he had lost the work as a result so didn't need them. He complained again and ended up having to send them back and chase for a refund. All because the person who took the complaint didn't listen properly to what the customer needed and so their solution didn't put the customer in the same position that they would have been!

When you phone:

1. Summarise the main points of the complaint and ask the customer to confirm that you are correct

2. Clearly explain your proposal and why you feel it addresses each point – if there are several points, it's best to address each one in turn and ask the customer to confirm they are happy the point has been addressed before moving onto the next one. This makes it easier for the customer to follow, and has an added benefit of getting the customer into the habit of agreeing, so they are much more likely to agree that the overall complaint has been resolved.

3. Ask if they are happy with your proposal. If not, then you need to ask why and either amend your proposal (if you can) or explain that further investigation is needed.

4. If they are happy, apologise again that they had to complain but that you're glad it is resolved to their satisfaction.

5. Finally, explain clearly what will happen next and when.

If you can't reach the customer on the phone, write or e-mail to them explaining that you think you can resolve their complaint and ask them to phone you.

And finally, don't forget to write to the customer as final confirmation.

Questions to ask yourself:

1. Do we always review the solution we are offering the customer to make sure we have answered all the points?

2. Do we always try to phone the customer?

3. Do we send a written confirmation?

Chapter 8

Learning from complaints

As I mentioned earlier in the book, customer complaints are a great source of customer feedback. Yes, it may be a difficult message sometimes, normally delivered with emotion, and yes, sometimes you may feel that the customer has blown things out of proportion. Remember though, one of my favourite quotations (from Maya Angelou) – "People will forget what you said, people will forget what you did, but people will never forget how you made them feel".

And that's why handling complaints properly will ultimately turn complaining customers into advocates for your brand. We all know that everyone makes mistakes, and the important thing is to learn from them (and hopefully not to repeat them).

Learning from complaints has 3 key phases:

First, make sure that you investigate the complaint thoroughly and that, as well as satisfying the customer, you really understand the root cause – the exact reason or reasons why it happened.

It's normally either:

- Something that went wrong or
- A policy or process that you have which is business rather than customer focused
- A communication problem.

Communication is the hardest to understand because it's not always immediately obvious that it was the problem – it tends to be the root cause of complaints where you at first feel that the customer's complaint was not justified. Try and get a third party opinion – ask someone who doesn't know your business well to read the communication and tell you what they think it means.

Second, when you are sure you understand the root cause, put a plan together to make changes so it won't happen again. Don't assume that you have all the answers – involving staff normally works well, and asking the customer who complained if the change you are proposing is right from their point of view is very powerful and helps to turn them into an advocate. Make sure you deliver the change – don't just plan it!

Third, tell your customers about the changes you have made – and why you made them. Many businesses choose not to do this – mainly because they don't want customers to realise that they are not perfect. Surprise news – they already know that!

Many large organisations only started to tell customers about the complaints they were receiving when their Regulator forced them to – and that's not a good position to be in!

Being open and honest with customers is a key part of building a good, long term relationship with them. Admitting to your mistakes and showing that you have learned from them is very powerful in helping to strengthen your relationship with your customers further – giving you happy customers who stay with you longer, buy more from you and refer others to you!

Questions to ask yourself:

1. Do we learn from customer complaints?
2. Do we ask customers if we are making the right change?
2. Do we demonstrate to customers that we have changed?

Nigel Greenwood

Nigel Greenwood has over 30 years' experience in designing and delivering great customer service for all sizes and types of business – covering complaint handling and resolution, sales, marketing, product design, channel development, administration and retention. Although he describes himself as "just a simple Yorkshireman", with over 20 years spent working for large corporates, his skill lies in being able to quickly understand how a business process works, how it impacts customers and how to make it simpler and better!

In 2014 he set up Simply Customer, which specialises in mapping customer journeys to show where businesses are losing sales, customers or generating queries and complaints, then redesigning the journeys and helping the business to deliver the change, giving them more, happier customers who buy more and stay longer. They also help businesses to continually monitor customer satisfaction and feedback, making sure that they continue to deliver great service and profits

You can contact Nigel at **nigel@simplycustomer.co.uk**, call 0113 892 1213 or connect with him on LinkedIn.

BITE-SIZED
BOOKS

The most successful people all share an ability to focus on what really matters, keeping things understandable and simple. MBAs, metrics and methodologies have their place, but when we are faced with a new business challenge most of us need quick guidance on what matters most, from people who have been there before and who can show us where to start. As Stephen Covey famously said, "The main thing is to keep the main thing, the main thing".

But what exactly is the main thing?

We created Bite-Sized books to help answer precisely that question crisply and quickly, working with writers who are experienced, successful and, of course, engaging to read.

The brief? Distil the *main things* into a book that can be read by an intelligent non-expert comfortably in around 60 minutes. Make sure the book provides the reader with specific tools, ideas and plenty of examples drawn from real life and business. Be a virtual mentor.

Bite-Sized Books don't cover every eventuality, but they are written from the heart by successful people who are happy to share their experience with you and give you the benefit of their success.

Printed in Great Britain
by Amazon